INVADERS FROM EARTH

INVASIVE PLANT SPECIES

Richard Spilsbury

PowerKiDS press™

New York

Published in 2015 by **The Rosen Publishing Group**
29 East 21st Street, New York, NY 10010

Library of Congress Cataloging-in-Publication Data

Spilsbury, Richard, 1963-
  Invasive plant species / Richard Spilsbury.
      pages cm. – (Invaders from earth)
  Includes index.
  ISBN 978-1-4994-0067-0 (pbk.)
  ISBN 978-1-4994-0037-3 (6 pack)
  ISBN 978-1-4777-7398-7 (library binding)
  1. Invasive plants—Juvenile literature. I. Title.
  II. Series: Spilsbury, Richard, 1963- Invaders from earth
  SB613.5.S69 2015
  581.6'2—dc23

                                        2014027645

Produced for Rosen by Calcium
Editors for Calcium: Sarah Eason and Robyn Hardyman
Designer: Paul Myerscough

Photo credits: Cover: Shutterstock: Four Oaks; Inside: Dreamstime: 24–25, Darius Baužys 19b, Echidna 13t, Claire Fulton 13b, Gardendreamer 29t, Afonskaya Irina 16t, Kcho 26b, Keith Spaulding 1, 7t, Lightscribe 6-7, Maljalen 14b, Dave Nelson 28b, Antonio Oquias 25b, Petarneychev 23t, Kris Petkong 24b, Marc Poveda 16b, Warren Price 9b, Mauro Rodrigues 16-17, Jason P Ross 8-9, Ben Smith 17t, Gerald Tang 23b, Jeffrey Van Daele 10t, Whiskybottle 15t, Zaramira 11b; Shutterstock: Binio 10-11, Blulz60 6b, Dontpoke 20b, Draga 22-23, Martin Fowler 14-15, Arnon Fueangphiban 20-21, Filip Fuxa 28-29, Rob Hainer 7b, Joloei 20t, Trevor Kelly 21b, Dan Kosmayer 10b, LeeMarUSA 27t, Lucky Business 26-27, Phillip Minnis 12-13, Ruud Morijn Photographer 2-3, 18-19, 30-31, 32, Christian Musat 9t, Noppharat 25t, Jay Ondreicka 19t, Photodiem 29b, Jason Patrick Ross 8b, V Schlichting 4b, Shutterschock 4t, Sihasakprachum 5, Paco Toscano 27b, Bonnie Watton 4-5; Wikimedia Commons: D Carlson 12b, Ivar Leidus 18b, 22b, MdE at Wikimedia Commons, CC-BY-SA 3.0 German 15b.

Manufactured in the United States of America

CPSIA Compliance Information: Batch CW15PK: For Further Information contact
Rosen Publishing, New York, New York at 1-800-237-9932

CONTENTS

WHAT ARE PLANT INVADERS?

Alien invaders are taking over Earth. These invaders do not come from another planet. Instead, they are plants brought into a country from elsewhere. The plants spread, taking over and causing serious problems for people and wildlife.

On the Attack

Some plant invaders grow alongside local plants and provide flowers for our parks and yards or food for our plates. Others may grow bigger or faster than local plants. They often spread unchecked because there are few or no animals that eat them. This allows invaders to take over land relatively quickly.

PLANTS FOR FOOD

4

Getting Around

How do plants get around? They invade new areas in different ways. People bring some plants into a country on purpose to grow for food, flowers, or other uses. Some plants are introduced by accident. For example, seeds can stick to a traveler's clothes or to a vehicle's wheels.

The Norway maple tree is a useful and attractive alien **species** that causes no harm. It has been introduced to parks in many parts of the world.

SPREADING SEEDS

INVADER ANALYSIS

The Global Invasive Species Programme (GISP) states that there are 316 **invasive** plants around the world putting **native** wildlife at risk in places where the invasive plants are not naturally found.

KUDZU

Kudzu is an incredible plant that can crawl, climb, and coil as it spreads over land, vehicles, and even houses! This vine is native to China, but it is now found all over the United States.

The Vine that Ate the South!

Kudzu is called "the vine that ate the South" because it covers so much land in the southern United States. In the 1930s, farmers planted kudzu to stop soil erosion. That is when wind and rain wear away areas of soil without any plants. Since then, kudzu spread like wildfire.

ROAD CLOSED

INVADER ANALYSIS

Kudzu can grow 1 foot (30 cm) a day and up to 100 feet (30 m) in a season. Its huge roots can weigh more than 100 pounds (45 kg). Up to 30 vines grow from one main root.

KILLER VINES!

SMOTHERED!

Creeping Killer

Kudzu vines have long stems that creep across land and climb upward. Kudzu kills native plants by blocking the light they need to make food. It also weighs down trees until they break. When kudzu grows up power lines, it causes power outages!

A kudzu plant in flower. The plants grow quickly, covering trees, fences, houses, and road signs in a blanket of leaves.

GARLIC MUSTARD

This alien invader was brought to the United States by early European settlers. It was used in cooking and as a medicine.

Woodland Weed

Garlic mustard grows rapidly in forests, roadsides, riverbanks, and backyards. It spreads like a green carpet, stealing light, water, and **nutrients** from native plants. In 10 years, it can replace all the native wildflowers in a forest. This threatens the butterflies that lay their eggs on those plants.

Garlic mustard seeds can lie for 5 years in the soil before growing and rapidly taking over areas of land.

Super Seeds

Garlic mustard spreads quickly because of its seeds. In May, its white flowers produce hundreds of seeds. When deer, squirrels, and other animals brush past the plants, the seeds stick to their fur. The seeds drop off and grow in new places.

FLOWERS

WHITE-TAILED DEER

EARTH UNDER ATTACK

In the United States, garlic mustard has no natural enemies. The white-tailed deer even helps it grow. This deer does not like the taste of garlic mustard, so it eats more native plants, which clears land for more garlic mustard to grow!

WATER HYACINTH

Water hyacinth is a beautiful plant that brightens ponds with its purple flowers. It is also one of the world's worst water weeds!

Fast Growth

Water hyacinth originally came from South America, where competing plants and natural enemies control its growth. In Africa and the United States, it spreads much quicker. This fast-growing plant can double in size in under 2 weeks. Its seeds travel long distances on the feet of waterbirds and on boats.

Water hyacinth can grow up to 3 feet (1 m) high.

Deadly Damage

When water hyacinth spreads, it stops light from reaching underwater plants and animals. It also blocks pipes that farmers use to water plants and special pipes that carry water away from land to prevent floods. Mosquitoes like to live where water hyacinth takes over, and in places such as Africa, these insects spread a disease called malaria.

MOSQUITO

LAKE VICTORIA

EARTH UNDER ATTACK

Water hyacinth almost ruined Lake Victoria's fishing industry in Uganda, Africa. Floating mats of water hyacinth grew so thick that fishing boats could not get through. They also stopped native plants from growing underwater, so fish could not feed and **reproduce**.

11

BLACK WATTLE

Black wattle is a beautiful but deadly tree. It is one of the world's worst invader plants in the United States, South Africa, Europe, and Asia.

Toughest Tree

Black wattle is native to Australia, but it was introduced to Africa, South America, and Europe for its **bark**. The bark contains a lot of tannin, which people use to turn animal skins into leather. Black wattle seeds have a tough, water-repellent **seed coat**. They can survive in soil for 50 years!

Black wattle flowers can produce thousands of tiny seeds that grow into more trees.

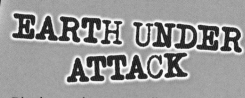

EARTH UNDER ATTACK

Black wattle is virtually unstoppable! Its seeds can survive fires, floods, and droughts. Fire triggers all the seeds in an area to grow at once!

SEED COATS

BLACK WATTLE

Plants Under Threat

Black wattles can grow to 90 feet (27 m), with a huge crown of leaves at the top. This blocks light from plants below. Black wattle robs other plants of water by sucking it all up from the soil. In many areas, black wattle is killing **indigenous** plants.

JAPANESE KNOTWEED

In many parts of the world, gardeners are at war. They are fighting the relentless attack of the Japanese knotweed, a plant that can spread up to 3 feet (1 m) a month!

GARDEN PEST

INVADER ANALYSIS

People spend a fortune getting rid of Japanese knotweed. In London, England, it reportedly cost $120 million to remove it from land where the 2012 Olympic Games were held.

Underground Attack

These plants are silent invaders. They reproduce from underground roots called **rhizomes**, instead of seeds. The roots spread unseen below the surface before new plants pop up.

JAPANESE KNOTWEED FLOWERS

If you dig up Japanese knotweed, it can regrow from a pea-sized piece of root.

Super Weed

This super weed is native to Japan, where natural enemies control it. However, in countries like the United Kingdom, it is such a pest that planting or dumping it can lead to jail or a fine! It takes space from indigenous plants, and its strong, long roots can crack concrete and damage houses, walls, sidewalks, and roads.

15

GIANT REEDS

The giant reed is a monster grass plant! It invades riverbanks and damp ground, and its canelike clumps form areas that are many feet wide.

GIANT REEDS

Robust Roots

Giant reed is native to Eastern Asia but has been grown around the world for walking sticks, fishing poles, and more. It spreads from thick, knobbly rhizomes that form giant root masses underground. **Stands** of giant reeds are so dense that they kill native plants, and the wildlife that rely on those plants decline.

WOODY STEMS

Crimes in California

In California, giant reeds are causing giant problems. They have replaced local plants such as native willows, which provided shelter and food for the yellow-billed cuckoo and other animals. The giant reed changes the flow of water in rivers and streams, which affects wildlife, such as the arroyo toad.

The giant reed's tube-like stems are used as reeds in the mouthpieces of woodwind instruments such as clarinets.

INVADER ANALYSIS

The giant reed grows incredibly quickly. It can grow 4 inches (10 cm) per day and reach a height of 25 feet (8 m) in 12 months. Its flat leaves can be 2 feet (60 cm) long and 3 inches (8 cm) wide!

PURPLE LOOSESTRIFE

Purple loosestrife's nicknames—beautiful killer or marsh monster—tell you all you need to know about this plant! Since the nineteenth century, when European settlers brought it to plant in North America, it has crowded out local plants and wildlife.

Marsh Monster

Purple loosestrife spreads far and wide because each plant can produce up to three million seeds every year in its spikes of reddish-purple flowers. The seeds are small and light and travel far in the wind to grow in new places.

PURPLE LOOSESTRIFE

Beautiful Killer

Purple loosestrife forms thick patches across marshes and other areas with damp soil, such as riverside fields. There it crowds out local plants such as cattails. This reduces the number of insects, birds, and other animals that rely on those local plants for food, shelter, and nesting material to survive.

WETLAND NUISANCE

Some people use weevils and beetles to eat and control purple loosestrife.

INVADER ANALYSIS

Around 470,000 acres (190,200 ha) of wetlands, marshes, fields, and riverbanks in North America are affected by purple loosestrife each year. People spend millions of dollars trying to control it.

19

SIAM WEED

Siam weed grows quickly to form high, dense, tangled thickets that prevent other plants from growing. It is a nuisance on farms and even helps wildfires spread.

Vicious Weed

Siam weed spreads widely and grows quickly. Its thick growth takes light, nutrients, and space from native plants that local animals rely on for food. It also kills cattle that eat it. In fact, it kills around 3,000 cattle a year in the Philippines.

Siam weed is soft when young, but gets tough and woody with age. Then it burns quickly and makes fires spread fast.

SIAM WEED

Slash and Burn?

Siam weed is native to Central America. It was introduced into India as a decorative plant in the 1840s, from where it spread to parts of Asia, Africa, and the Pacific. It is difficult to get rid of because it grows back quickly after burning or cutting.

EARTH UNDER ATTACK

In parts of South Africa, Siam weed covers land with mats of roots, making nest building difficult for some animals, such as the Nile crocodile. The plants also create shade that makes eggs cooler and may prevent the babies inside from developing.

CROCODILE EGGS

LEAFY SPURGE

In some places, leafy spurge is called wolf's milk. That is because it contains a substance that makes some animals sick!

The Root of the Problem

Native to Europe and parts of Asia, leafy spurge is now found all over the world. Its large roots take over huge areas of soil, robbing other plants of the water and nutrients they need. It is one of the first plants to emerge in the spring, so it shades other plants, blocking the light they need to grow.

Leafy spurge displaces many native plants.

Wolf's Milk

In fields, leafy spurge can take the place of up to three-quarters of native grasses. These grasses are important food for farm animals. However, leafy spurge's milky sap contains ingenol, a substance that causes sickness and diarrhea in animals that eat it.

CATTLE UNDER THREAT

LEAFY SPURGE

INVADER ANALYSIS

Leafy spurge has spread to more than 5 million acres (2,023,428 ha) of grazing land in the northern Great Plains, United States. The cost of controlling the plant and the loss of available grazing grasses costs more than $100 million yearly.

COGON GRASS

Cogon grass is one of the top-ten worst weeds in the world! Once this alien invader arrives in an area, it is almost impossible to get rid of.

Greedy Grass

Cogon grass can grow in almost every **habitat**, from dry fields to riverbanks. It has large roots that spread widely, forming thick stands that crowd out the local plants many animals eat. In Florida, cogon grass stands can destroy the habitat of rare animals such as gopher tortoises and indigo snakes.

COGON GRASS

EARTH UNDER ATTACK

Cogon grass burns 400°F (205°C) hotter than native plants. Flames in a cogon grass fire can be more than 20 feet (6 m). The grass then grows back before other plants can grow.

Pine Problems

Dry cogon catches fire easily, and these fires can destroy trees. Cogon grass roots release chemicals into the soil that stop plant seeds from growing. It can turn a forest full of wildlife to grassland with far fewer plants and animals.

DRY GRASSES

Cogon grass is useful in some places, where it is used as roofing material, but it is a pest in more than 70 countries.

25

PRICKLY PEAR

Prickly pear is a spiky cactus that can grow taller than a man! It is native to Central America but has invaded other regions. It is such a problem in Australia that it is called the "pest pear."

Australia's Worst Weed

Early settlers planted prickly pears in Australia as spiky boundaries to control cattle. However, prickly pears soon took over valuable farmland. In 1926, the government had Argentinian cactus moths released. The moths laid eggs in the cactus, and the caterpillars that hatched ate the plants. In 10 years, the caterpillars cleared 25 million acres (10,117,141 ha) of prickly pear!

People eat the pear-shaped fruit that grow on this cactus, but the spikes can hurt people and animals.

Cunning Cactus

Prickly pears can survive in hot, dry weather longer than other plants because they store water in their stems. Their sharp spikes stop animals from eating them for this water. Birds and animals eat the fruit and spread the seeds in their droppings.

PRICKLY PEAR

FRUIT EATER

EARTH UNDER ATTACK

The cactus moth saved Australia but is ruining parts of the United States. There these caterpillars also feed on the rare semaphore cactus, and there is a danger that this native plant could soon die out as a result.

SOS: SAVE OUR SPECIES!

Plant invaders are a serious threat to entire **ecosystems**. How can we stop these aliens?

Species Under Threat

Most plant-eating insects eat only certain native plants. So, when a plant invader takes over from local plants, the insects decline. When there are fewer insects, there is less food for birds and other animals. This is bad for people, too, because we need a variety of living things to keep the natural world healthy.

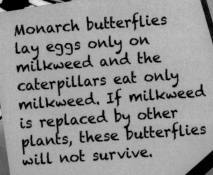

Monarch butterflies lay eggs only on milkweed and the caterpillars eat only milkweed. If milkweed is replaced by other plants, these butterflies will not survive.

EARTH UNDER ATTACK

Many scientists think **global warming** is making Earth hotter. This could help invasive plants spread. For example, North American common ragweed is spreading farther north, and this plant triggers hay fever and other allergies.

RAGWEED POLLEN

What Can Be Done?

Scientists are always searching for ways to stop plant invaders. For example, just 3 years after their release, weevils had wiped out more than half of the water hyacinth on Lake Victoria. We can plant more native species to provide shelter and food for native wildlife. However, the best way to stop plants from invading is to never introduce them!

SCIENTIST AT WORK

GLOSSARY

bark The tough covering of a tree trunk.

ecosystems All the living things in an area and the place where they live and find food.

erosion The wearing away of rock or land.

global warming The general increase in temperatures on Earth.

habitat A place where plants or animals live.

indigenous Born in or belonging to a particular place.

invasive Tending to spread quickly and cause damage to other things around it.

native Born in or belonging to a particular place.

nutrients Substances living things obtain from their food and that they need in order to live.

reproduce To make babies.

rhizomes Thick plant stems that grow underground.

seed coat The outer covering that protects parts inside the seed.

species Types of living things.

stands Groups of tall plants or trees.

FURTHER READING

Books

Baird Rattini, Kristin. *National Geographic Readers: Seed to Plant*. Des Moines, IA: National Geographic Children's Books, 2014.

Farrell, Courtney. *Plants Out of Place* (Let's Explore Science). Vero Beach, FL: Rourke Publishing Group, 2010.

Gould, Margee. *Poisonous Plants* (The Strangest Plants on Earth). New York, NY: Rosen Publishing Group, 2012.

Websites

Due to the changing nature of Internet links, PowerKids Press has developed an online list of websites related to the subject of this book. This site is updated regularly. Please use this link to access the list:
www.powerkidslinks.com/ife/plant

INDEX